FAMOUS MOVIE MONSTERS™

MEET THE CREATURE FROM THE BLACK LAGOON

The Rosen Publishing Group, Inc.
New York

BRENT PETERSON

For Parker and Maddux, my two favorite creatures

Published in 2005 by The Rosen Publishing Group, Inc.
29 East 21st Street, New York, NY 10010

First Edition

Library of Congress Cataloging-in-Publication Data

Peterson, Brent.
Meet the Creature from the Black Lagoon/by Brent Peterson.—1st ed.
     p. cm.—(Famous movie monsters)
Filmography:
Includes bibliographical references and index.
ISBN 1-4042-0272-2 (lib. bdg.)
1. Creature from the Black Lagoon (Motion picture)
I. Title. II. Series.
PN1997.C853P48 2005
791.43'72–dc22

                                        2004020487

Manufactured in the United States of America

On the cover: The Creature from the Black Lagoon

CONTENTS

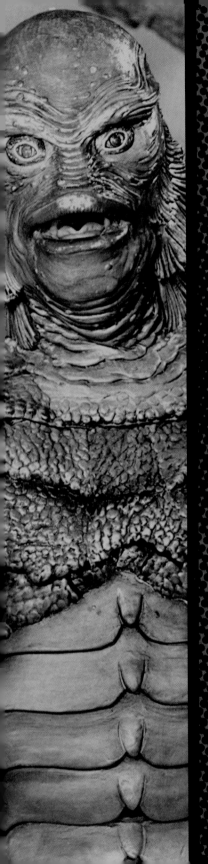

CHAPTER 1

CREATURE FROM THE BLACK LAGOON

On an archaeological dig, deep in the Amazon jungle, Dr. Carl Maia makes a disturbing discovery—a fossil, shaped like a human hand but with webbing and sharp claws! Is it the remains of some prehistoric man or that of some large fish? Or both?

Members of his team crowd around him to examine the piece. They take pictures to record their find and ponder the fossil's true origins.

"It must have been a real killer," a team member suggests, pointing to the fossil's deadly claws.

Whatever it was, Dr. Maia knows he has unearthed something important. Perhaps the hand belonged to a long-extinct race of man or animal species—something mankind never even knew existed? Either way, he knows his best chance of learning its origins is back at the Marine Biology Institute, where he can study it more closely with the other scientists. Ordering the others to stay behind and guard the digging site, Dr. Maia boards a boat and speeds off down the jungle river and back to the institute.

Curious scientists Dr. David Reed (Richard Carlson), his assistant Kay (Julia Adams), Dr. Mark Williams (Richard Denning), and Dr. Edwin Thompson (Whit Bissell) examine what looks to be a fossil of a webbed human hand with claws.

Back at the dig site, no one notices the bubbles rising from the murky waters nearby. Unnoticed, a hand slowly rises to the surface. The grisly hand has webbing and sharp claws, just like the fossil recently uncovered!

At the institute, a team of scientists joins Dr. Maia in examining the strange fossil. Dr. Mark Williams, the head of the institute, quickly realizes what an amazing discovery this is. He, too, is perplexed by its origins. Dr. Edwin Thompson is also wowed by the find, theorizing that the hand might be a "missing link" in the evolutionary chain between land and sea animals. Dr. David Reed and his assistant, Kay Lawrence, are also present. Together, the group wonders if even greater fossil samples can be discovered along the bottom of the riverbed. It is agreed that the group will lead an expedition back to the area in order to solve the mystery and, perhaps, unearth even greater pieces of human history.

However, finding a boat to take the scientists back up the river to the dig site proves surprisingly difficult. Many of the local riverboat captains are fearful of heading that far up the river. Tales of water monsters who dwell in those parts terrify the locals. It takes some convincing, but one boat owner does finally agree to take them. Captain Lucas and his boat, the *Rita*, will do it.

Back at the dig site, the two remaining scientists, Luis and Manuel, sit nervously inside their tent. Night has fallen, and the jungle is full of strange sounds tonight. They, too, have heard stories of monsters in these parts. And after finding the strange fossil hand, they're starting to believe them.

Without warning, the night grows quiet and still. What could make the lively jungle grow so silent? Then, they hear a most terrible sound, a growl like no man's or beast's, followed by the sound of splashing. It is as if some terrible

The clawed and scaly Creature proves he is as adept on land as he is in the water. The Creature's look was inspired by the gold statue given out at the Academy Awards, known as the Oscar. Makeup artist Bud Westmore based many of his ideas for the monster on what he thought the Oscar would look like if it were a frightening creature.

beast is coming out of the water, heading toward the tent. The two men's worst fears are confirmed as a horrible reptile-like creature enters through the tent's opening. The ghastly Creature stands before them! It's covered head to toe in green, scaly skin. Gills line the beast's neck and lead to its ghastly head where two terrifying dark eyes stare at them.

What is it? What does it want? One of the men screams in terror as the Creature comes toward them. And then they see those claws, those ferocious claws, reaching out, coming ever closer!

Fearing for his life, one of the men tosses a nearby kerosene lamp on the Creature. The beast lets out a pained scream as the kerosene burns its skin and momentarily halts the monster's approach. The fire spreads to the floor and walls of the tent, quickly engulfing it in flames. The Creature is hurt but still comes toward the men, lunging, reaching, clawing! The jungle is awash in screams.

*   *   *

The next morning, the boat arrives at camp with the scientists from the institute. They find a burned-down tent and the lifeless bodies of Luis and Manuel. Upon close inspection, it appears both men died not of burns from the fire but rather at the hands of some ferocious animal. They were savagely attacked!

After seeing the fallen men, an ominous feeling takes hold over the group. However, their mission is too important to stop now. They can't turn back. They must conduct their search for more clues and perhaps a solution to the origins of the strange fossil.

For more than a week, the team conducts a thorough search of the dig site without any luck. Some members of the team use scuba gear to search the water. Others dig along the shoreline. Someone suggests they look farther upstream. The suggestion draws caution from the boat's captain. He knows all too well of where they speak. Upstream is a remote area that the locals call the Black Lagoon.

"It is said to be a paradise," the captain explains, "but no one has ever come back from there alive to prove it."

The head scientist, Dr. Williams, sneers at the notion of monsters and curses. He orders the boat upriver so they can resume their search. The captain reluctantly agrees and begins navigating the *Rita* cautiously through the narrow passages and dark waters to the Black Lagoon. Once there, Dr. Williams and David put on their diving gear to have a look under the water. Little do they suspect they are not alone—the gruesome Creature lurks in the water's depths, watching them as they examine the rocks along the water's bottom. The Creature's gills allow it to breathe underwater, with no apparent difficulty. It does nothing but watch—for now.

Later, Kay decides to take a swim in the Black Lagoon. The Creature studies her, too, from the watery depths, transfixed as she swims above. The Creature is curious by what he sees. Has it ever seen a human female before? It wants a closer look. As Kay returns to the boat, the Creature nearly catches up to her. Kay struggles to get up the ladder and the Creature begins rocking the boat, alerting everyone on board. One crew member notices something caught in the net attached to the boat. This is no ordinary fish! When the crew finally manages to pull the mangled net from the water, all that is found is a long, vicious claw. They are not alone in the Black Lagoon.

Dr. Williams is ecstatic at the discovery of the claw. The Creature must be somewhere in the lagoon! He grabs a speargun with hopes of killing the beast. "If we can kill it and take it out of here, we'll become famous," he explains to the others.

David argues that the mission is not to kill the Creature but to study it. They are scientists, not hunters! However, Dr. Williams doesn't listen. As head of the expedition, he orders David into his diving gear to help hunt the Creature.

The dark waters of the lagoon make it difficult for them to see. Neither man sees the Creature until it suddenly appears right before them. Dr. Williams fires his speargun and hits the Creature, who retreats into a hole within the rocks down below. The two men return to the boat to tell the others.

That night, as the crew sleeps, the Creature creeps on board the *Rita* and pulls one of the deckhands overboard, drowning him. The man's screams wake the crew, who are now more terrified than ever. Captain Lucas devises a plan involving rotenone, a chemical he often uses to stun and capture fish. They will use it to subdue the Creature. The scientists watch as Captain Lucas fills the lagoon with the rotenone. It sends scores of stunned fish to the surface but, alas, no Creature.

Later, a loud noise erupts on shore. A crewman shines a light in that direction: the Creature has returned! David and Dr. Williams rush onto land after it, with spearguns in

The Creature creeps up on the *Rita*'s crew. Two actors were required to play the Creature. Ben Chapman played the monster on land, and former Olympic swimmer Ricou Browning played it in the water. The two men were of varying heights, though viewers are not able to see the difference on-screen.

hand, following it to a nearby cave. They fire the weapons and wound the Creature, who flees the cave only to find Kay on the shore. A brave deckhand attacks the Creature but suffers the full fate of the wounded Creature's fury. During the struggle, however, the others manage to subdue the beast and capture it with a net. They construct a cage made of wood and keep the Creature there. Their suspicions have been confirmed—the Creature is indeed part man but breathes with gills, as a fish does. They start to examine it up close but fail to realize just how strong it is until it's too late. The Creature breaks free of its prison and vanishes back into the murky deep of the Black Lagoon.

David and the crew beg Dr. Williams to let them leave and let the Creature go in peace. However, Dr. Williams is more convinced than ever he wants to hunt down the Creature. Captain Lucas, tired of taking orders, pulls a knife and holds it to the doctor's throat. "I say we're going home," he insists. The knife is a persuasive argument.

The team decides to make a hasty retreat back up the small channel. But shockingly, a fallen tree blocks the boat's path. Was it some sort of a trap? Before the crew knows for sure, the Creature crawls on board for another attack. One of the crewmen fires his gun, and the Creature disappears back into the lagoon. The team then focuses its attention to dislodging the tree using the boat's winch. The only way to move the tree is to enter the water and tie a line around it. The Creature, no doubt, will be waiting.

Dr. Williams and David return to the water only to be attacked. This time, Dr. Williams, who had wanted nothing more than to kill the Creature, perishes during the fight. David barely escapes with his own life. On board, the remaining scientists devise one last plan to get the boat free. They will

The Creature falls in love with the beautiful Kay Lawrence (Julia Adams). Many other famous horror movies, such as *Dracula*, *The Mummy*, and *King Kong*, also feature monsters who fall in love with humans.

Dr. Maia (Antonio Moreno) and Captain Lucas (Nestor Paiva) fire shots at the Creature, saving David and Kay from the menacing monster. Though the Creature is wounded at the end of the film, it is allowed to live and return to the Black Lagoon, setting the stage for the sequels to come.

use the last of the rotenone to stun the Creature if he should attack David underwater again.

David enters the water and repels the Creature with the rotenone. This buys him enough time to fasten a cable around the fallen tree, allowing the boat's winch to pull it out of their way. Their joy, however, is short-lived as the Creature sneaks on board and captures Kay. Was it her it wanted all along?

The Creature flees with Kay back to its cave lair with David following close behind. He doesn't want to hurt the Creature and only wishes to free Kay. David and the Creature wrestle, fighting for dear life, as the Creature's sharp claws reach out to David's throat.

Suddenly, gunshots ring out, fired by Dr. Maia and Captain Lucas. The Creature is badly wounded. It staggers back to the lagoon.

David still wants to avoid killing the Creature. He has, strangely, sensed the humanity in it. "It had attacked only when it felt threatened by human beings," he says to the remaining scientists, as he carries Kay to safety. David asks the men to lower their weapons as the stumbling, wounded Creature falls into the water and slowly sinks back into the Black Lagoon.

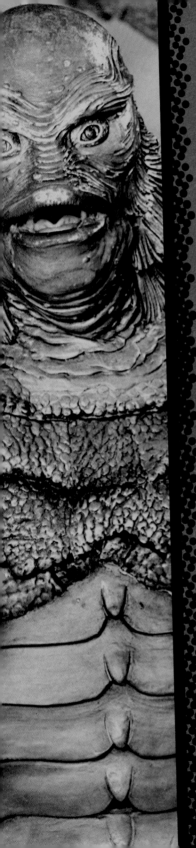

CHAPTER 2

THE CREATURE GOES HOLLYWOOD

The 1950s was a great decade for monster movies. It was also an era filled with paranoia and anxiety for many Americans. World War II (1939–1945) had recently ended, punctuated with the dropping of two devastating atomic bombs. This established a wave of fear concerning atomic energy and its horrifying powers. To worsen matters, the Cold War had begun. The Cold War (1947–1991) was a decades-long standoff between the world's two superpowers, the United States and the Soviet Union. America was ever fearful of the intentions of its Soviet enemy. In short, Americans had a lot of nervous energy, which is probably why the safe terror found at the movie theater watching a good, scary movie became so popular.

During the atomic age, monsters and aliens seemed to dominate the screen in a wave of what were called B movies, films that were made quickly with little to no budget. The special effects often left much to be desired, but they were considered good fun during those times. In the midst of all of this, a scaly, clawed "gill-man" known only as the Creature would take its place among the most popular and most beloved scary icons ever. In a time when many monster movies were anything less than memorable, *Creature from the Black Lagoon* took hold of the American psyche.

CREATING THE CREATURE

The job of creating the Creature's look fell to well-known Hollywood makeup artist Bud Westmore, who had a strange source of inspiration for its design. Westmore was best known for his work in *Abbott and Costello Meet Frankenstein* (1948), *The Life of Riley* (1949), and *It Came from Outer Space* (1953), among countless other movies over a thirty-five-year career. Before creating the Creature, he was nominated for an Academy Award as a makeup artist and wondered what the award itself—a gold statue of a faceless man known as an Oscar—would look like as a menacing creature. He decided to add claws, gills, and

As the flashy posters show, *Creature from the Black Lagoon* was similar to the many B movie horror flicks that dominated screens in the 1950s. However, the film was a standout in the genre and became a horror classic.

Films such as *(clockwise, from top left) Fiend Without a Face* (1958), *The Thing* (1951), *Them!* (1954), and *Day the World Ended* (1956) are prime examples of the popularity of the monster movie among 1950s audiences.

scales to the basic shape and got to work designing a costume for the upcoming film.

As the story goes, the film's would-be producer, William Alland, promised to deliver a script once a compelling Creature was created. In those days, it was not unusual for scripts to be written quickly in order to capitalize on a good idea. The good idea, in this case, was that of a prehistoric water monster terrorizing a crew of scientists who enter its lair, the Black Lagoon. The idea wasn't exactly original, with many of the movie's exact same elements seen just a year before in the movie *The Beast from 20,000 Fathoms*. That particular movie was a hit with theatergoers. Alland wanted his company, Universal International (which later became Universal Studios), to work from the basic idea of a frightening creature lurking in the waters below.

Bud Westmore faced unusual challenges with the Creature's costume, however. He had a basic design in mind, but the costume and makeup would need to be both waterproof and durable enough to withstand plenty of action, including fight scenes and running. Hollywood was still in its infancy in terms of special effects and costume design. The costume for the Creature would be a unique combination that no one had experience with. As such, the idea of giving the Creature a mechanical tail was dropped because of the difficulty in making it work underwater. The other challenge was the Creature itself, who was said to be at least part human. This required the use of an actor to play the part, rather than relying on special effects or other moviemaking tricks to bring it to life. Whatever final design for the Creature Westmore and his team, including Jack Kevan, Bob Hickman, and Chris Mueller, came up with, it would need to be like nothing movies had ever seen before.

A DIFFERENT KIND OF MOVIEMAKING

Creature from the Black Lagoon, as it would be called, was going to be different in other respects as well. The screenplay,

Though the underwater photography required for *Creature from the Black Lagoon* was difficult for the actors and the camera crew to shoot, the scary underwater sequences are key to the film's lasting appeal. The underwater footage and special effects were highly impressive at the time of the film's release.

written by Harry Essex and Arthur A. Ross (taken from a story devised by Maurice Zimm), called for much of the action and photography to take place underwater. This would be another challenge in terms of filmmaking. Filming in water had numerous problems, not the least of which was the use of tricky underwater cameras and actors who may or may not have been skilled swimmers. One of the hallmarks of

Creature from the Black Lagoon is the underwater photography, shot by cinematographer Charles S. Welbourne. At times terrifying, at other times dreamy, the water footage was considered some of the best ever filmed at the time of the film's release in 1954. These effects were even made stronger when seen in the film's original format—3-D.

Creature from the Black Lagoon was originally filmed in 3-D, also known as three-dimensional. Three-dimensional moviemaking was a somewhat gimmicky process popular during the 1950s, especially in monster movies, and caused the actions on the screen to come alive. By wearing a special pair of card-

Three-dimensional films, which require that viewers wear a special pair of cardboard glasses, were very popular in the 1950s. Like many horror films of its time, *Creature from the Black Lagoon* was originally filmed in 3-D.

board glasses with special lenses, audience members would see the movie's images come alive as never before. Images appeared to jump off the screen. For instance, a car motoring across the movie screen in a 3-D movie might appear as if it were actually driving into the audience, which gave viewers quite a thrill. This was an especially useful

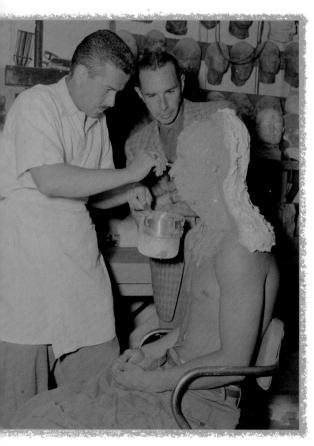

Makeup artists transform Ricou Browning into the Creature. Browning was an Olympic swimmer who could hold his breath for up to five minutes, an important skill to have when shooting scenes underwater.

technique for action-intense movies like *Creature from the Black Lagoon*.

FINDING THE CREATURE

Not just any actor could play the physically challenging part of the Creature. Therefore, the producers decided to get one actor for the action on land and another for the grueling underwater scenes. A young actor named Ben Chapman played the Creature on land, while Ricou Browning was the perfect person to handle the Creature's underwater scenes. An Olympic swimmer who could hold his breath for up to five minutes, Browning could handle the rigorous demands of such filming while looking like the Creature in its natural environment. As it turned out, Browning was so good as the Creature that he later made his mark in Hollywood as a well-known choreographer for underwater action scenes. He even went on to create the popular 1960s TV show *Flipper*, about a family and their faithful dolphin.

Costume designers constructed special rubber suits from a body mold set to the precise measurements of each man (Chapman was 6 feet 5 inches tall and Browning 5 feet 8 inches tall, but you couldn't tell the difference on-screen). Scales and claws were cemented into place, and the suits were colored green, like a reptile. The skintight suits gave the Creature a realistic look that many of the low-budget monster movies of the day definitely lacked. Browning's costume even had rubber air bladders behind the "gills" on the neck. These would fill up with air to simulate the Creature's breathing. The final cost for the Creature suit was $12,000, a fairly expensive undertaking at the time.

The fact that the Creature was human-sized added to its sense of believability as well. Most movie monsters of the time were far-fetched, like the towering Godzilla (who also debuted in 1954) or some crazy monster with tentacles and an alien brain.

PLAYING GAMES WITH THE AUDIENCE

In an effort to make the Creature appear more real, the studio hyped the Creature in its advertisements for the movie as "either the last remnant of a 15-million-year-old species, or has itself survived since the Devonian age. Substantially taller than the average human male, although never accurately measured. Approximately 300 pounds." The Creature was compared to "the African lungfish, which lives underwater during mating season, but breathes surface air when its lake habitat dries up."

Ben Chapman and Julia Adams have a laugh during the filming of *Creature from the Black Lagoon*. Though Adams would never match the success of *Creature* in her later work, she did forge a successful career in television and movies that spanned all the way into the 1990s.

THE CAST AND CREW

When it came time to appoint a director, the studio chose Jack Arnold. Although he had previously directed only a few films, one was rather noteworthy and soon to be a classic. A tale of hostile aliens looking to take over the world, *It Came from Outer Space* hit movie theaters in 1953 and was a smash hit for Arnold and the studio. He went on to have other horror hits, including *Revenge of the Creature* (the sequel to *Creature from the Black Lagoon*), *Tarantula*, *The Incredible Shrinking Man*, *The Space Children*, *Monster on the Campus*, and the Peter Sellers comedy *The Mouse that Roared*.

Veteran actors were brought in to play the lead roles, including Julia Adams (Kay Lawrence) and Richard Denning (Dr. Mark Williams), who was perhaps best known as the hero in the classic bug movie *The Black Scorpion*. Dr. David Reed was played by Richard Carlson, who had made a name for himself in Arnold's *It Came from Outer Space*. Each actor also had a stunt double to handle underwater scenes.

BEHIND THE SCENES

Every classic horror movie features its own special music, or score, as it's called in films. The score is a key element to set an emotional tone for the viewers. The right notes and chords can cause movie watchers to feel anxious, sad, or joyous—or just about any emotion in between. The score for *Creature* became one of the most famous—and recognizable—in the horror genre. It required the collective talents of a team of composers to come up with the tense, pulse-pounding score, including Joseph Gershenson and Henry Mancini, who went on to become one of the most famous composers in movies and television.

The movie itself was filmed on two locations. Wakulla State Park in Florida's panhandle played home to the Black Lagoon, where most of the water scenes were filmed. The rest of the film was shot at the Universal Studios lot in Hollywood, where filmmakers could better control the action.

AMERICA FALLS IN LOVE WITH THE CREATURE

Running just seventy-nine minutes in length and filmed in the traditional black-and-white style, as was customary of the time, *Creature from the Black Lagoon* exploded onto screens in 1954 and was an immediate hit with moviegoers, who felt both fear and sympathy for the lonesome yet horrific Creature. The original movie spawned two sequels and immediately propelled the Creature into the who's who of Hollywood monsters.

Despite the movie's somewhat corny dialogue and over-the-top action, the Creature itself was thought of as both sympathetic and complex, which added to its appeal. The fact that it scared almost everyone who watched the movie no doubt helped the film gain nationwide attention as a standout in the horror genre. Despite its vile actions, which included murder, mayhem, and kidnapping, the Creature is often seen as the movie's true victim. For many, the beast is not seen as a monster but rather as a symbol of mankind's aggression and conquest over the environment and one another. Because of the Creature's complex nature, the monster remains one of moviedom's most famous creations a half-century after its debut and has spawned countless imitators along the way.

CHAPTER 3

AMERICA LOVES ITS MONSTERS

As opposed to the well-known beginnings of such mainstay monsters as Dracula or Frankenstein, the origins of the Creature are not easily pegged down. Certainly, the climate of the 1950s Hollywood era had a lot to do with it.

During this time, studios seemed to spend more time chasing the latest fad and copying what successful movies had done than they did with coming up with something new. Throughout the decade, the monster movie was king, seen as a quick and easy movie formula and, therefore, often one resulting in high profits. Audience standards were usually pretty low, too. It seemed people were just looking for some good scares and maybe a laugh or two along the way. They came to expect less and less from these kinds of films. Movie theaters across the country were full of screenings of the latest ghoul, alien, or creature wreaking havoc. However, it wasn't until the 1954 release of *Creature from the Black Lagoon* that the term "Creature" would become synonymous with one unique Hollywood creation.

THE BEAST FROM 1953

Just a year before *Creature*'s release in 1954, America enjoyed watching *The Beast from 20,000 Fathoms* unleash its fury on the screen. The movie was a smash hit and was released among many other monster movies about atomic energy gone awry, hostile aliens, or the timeless exploits of proven monsters such as vampires and werewolves. However, *The Beast from 20,000 Fathoms* stood out from the pack of these run-of-the-mill monster flicks. The idea of a prehistoric sea creature terrorizing humans by crawling from the depths of the sea was just original enough to garner audience attention. Universal International noticed, too, and the film arguably became the greatest inspiration for its nameless water monster, known only as the Creature. Certainly, it's no mere coincidence that a year after *The Beast from 20,000 Fathoms* shocked moviegoers, *Creature from the Black Lagoon* debuted on the silver screen.

SOUTH AMERICAN LORE

Still, the Creature residing in the Black Lagoon was different. More man than monster, with an average size, the Creature seemed more like something Earth had forgotten. This was far different from the decade's other monsters, who were typically created in a laboratory or as a result of some freakish accident. Although not exactly probable, the thought that such a creature might be living in a South American river isn't so outlandish, is it? After all, every year people still hunt for the

The prehistoric sea creature turned terrorizing monster from *The Beast from 20,000 Fathoms* (1953) was a major inspiration for *Creature from the Black Lagoon*. *The Beast*'s success spurred Universal to develop its own horror movie about a menacing water creature.

legendary Loch Ness monster in Scotland or even Bigfoot, the hairy creature that supposedly haunts the American Northwest.

Producer William Alland was also said to have heard the frightening tales of a swamp monster living in the South American jungles and waterways, and this was part of the inspiration for his Black Lagoon tale. As legend had it, this "creature" was often described as part man, part alligator.

The fact that a similar Amazon setting was created for the film is worth mentioning. Others believe that *Creature from the Black Lagoon* itself was more influenced by author H. P. Lovecraft, who wrote a tale of strange creatures that never evolved from their amphibian stage. In his story entitled "The Shadow over Innsmouth," the author created a fictional town

LIKE THE APE BEFORE IT

Creature from the Black Lagoon also owes much to *King Kong* (1933), one of the most famous movies of the genre. Like the isolated Creature, the giant ape has proven to be a sympathetic character. Kong, too, has an unusual interest in the movie's leading lady, eventually capturing her and carrying her up the side of the Empire State Building in New York City before perishing at the hands of the human aggressors. The love story, subtly played in *Creature* with Julia Adams (Kay), is said to be one of the most enduring aspects of the story.

Creature from the Black Lagoon owes a large debt to *King Kong*, the definitive beauty-and-the-beast horror movie. Both films feature love stories between misunderstood monsters and beautiful women, and these romantic elements lend to the films' lasting appeal.

Featured above are alleged photos of the legendary creatures Bigfoot
(left) and the Loch Ness monster. Like these myths, which still manage to
capture the imaginations of people around the world, movie monsters have
an enduring popularity.

inhabited by green, watery creatures who hid their gills from
the rest of the world.

Still, like many movies of the time—and since—the
movie's success lies greatly in proven plot formulas and
moviemaking techniques. The fear of the unknown, whether it
is the unknown happenings on a distant planet or just life
below the water's murky surface, is always compelling material

to get people good and edgy. Embracing the proven notion that people often fear what they can't see—and don't understand—the Black Lagoon represents both of these things. Only in this movie—and ensuing sequels—these fears come true when the scaly Creature, with its razor-sharp claws and horrifying reptile face, surfaces from the depths.

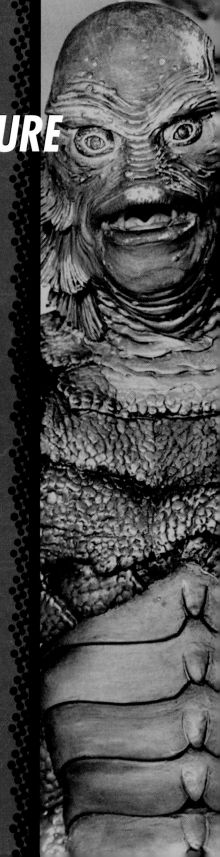

CHAPTER 4

LONG LIVE THE CREATURE

Just who is the hero of *Creature from the Black Lagoon*? For most viewers, it's dutiful David, who goes toe-to-toe with the Creature in tireless fashion. David also engages in an ongoing debate of ethics and scientific duty with the head of the scientific team, Dr. Williams, who becomes obsessed with killing the Creature. Is it any wonder that David ends up with the girl at the end? Still, the Creature is a compelling character in its own right and unquestionably carries the movie, as well as the following two sequels.

WHO IS THE REAL MONSTER?

In the same spirit as they see the monster in the 1931 classic *Frankenstein*, moviegoers often view the Creature as a persecuted victim, an animal only protecting itself from ever-encroaching humans. This dramatic turn, in which audiences actually feel sympathy for a gnarling, often ferocious gill-man, rests at the heart of the movie's longtime appeal and success. It is, after all, the eager scientists who invade and disrupt the Creature's world, not the other way around. It is the head of the institute himself, Dr. Williams, who seems to be the aggressor by demanding the team capture and kill the Creature on first sight. Is the doctor's seeming intolerance toward the Creature the real evil in this monster movie?

Despite the killing of much of the team, there is still the question of the Creature's true motivation: is it good or evil? Just what were the Creature's intentions in the beginning of the movie when it entered the scientist's tent? Was it out for blood or possibly just an understanding of a humankind it may never have encountered before? The Creature did kill two men, but was the Creature merely curious or on a rampage? It's just not clear, although the Creature's motives seem clear to the members of the scientific expedition convinced it is out to do the

Though the Creature is the villain in *Creature from the Black Lagoon,* he is also in some ways the victim. His love for Kay makes him a more sympathetic character than the average movie monster.

world harm. This belief then unleashes a chain of dark and disruptive events.

The script also relies on the beauty and the beast concept, in which a hideous monster (hideous by human standards, of course) is intrigued by a beautiful woman. In that respect, the movie owes part of its appeal to films such as *King Kong*, in which the gargantuan ape falls for the beautiful heroine only to be tragically killed. Perhaps America has a soft spot for a lovelorn monster?

Or maybe the Creature endures as a movie icon because it's a one-of-a-kind creation that captures the heart of moviegoers. It is no doubt terrifying to see a scaled being, with sharp claws and bulging eyeballs, rise out of the water. The webbed hands, the toadlike head, and the combination of both man and reptile all make for a pretty good scare. And people enjoy a good scare.

REVENGE OF THE CREATURE

Whatever the source of the movie's appeal, Universal Studios commissioned two more movies immediately following the successful launch of the first Creature flick. *Revenge of the Creature*, released in 1955 and once again directed by Jack Arnold, sees a second, obviously foolhardy group of scientists invade the lagoon. This answers the question of whether or not the Creature survived his gunshot wounds from the first movie. Ricou Browning, who played the Creature during the underwater scenes in the first movie, is the only member of the original cast to return to the sequel.

Ricou Browning returned to his role as the Creature for the sequel to *Creature from the Black Lagoon*, titled *Revenge of the Creature* (1955). In the film, the Creature is captured and placed in a Florida aquarium. Though it is not the most famous or acclaimed movie of the three Creature films, *Revenge of the Creature* was the most commercially successful.

This time, they not only manage to capture the Creature, they also relocate him to a Florida aquarium, where it is chained and onlookers can view him as a sort of shocking spectacle. But the most shocking thing of all is when the Creature escapes, much to the horror of the curious onlookers. In the sequel, the Creature again struggles with his emotions toward a new object of desire, the girlfriend of one of the scientists. In this movie, we see even more of the Creature's humanity as it realizes it can't return to its watery home with the woman for fear of drowning her. Once again, the movie ends with the Creature's apparent death. But again, rumors of its demise are premature, allowing it to return to the screen for yet another sequel.

THE CREATURE WALKS AMONG US

We learn in the third and final film, *The Creature Walks Among Us*, that the Creature did indeed survive its second run-in with the scientists but now lives in the swamps of Florida. Again, scientists pursue and capture it after wounding it badly. Extensive tests conclude the Creature is indeed probably exactly what audience members may have suspected all along—much more human than originally thought.

THE CREATURE SPAWNS A STAR

Revenge of the Creature, while a weak sequel, does have one major distinction for movie buffs. *Revenge of the Creature* was Hollywood mainstay Clint Eastwood's very first film. In the sequel, Eastwood is in a brief scene as one of the scientists. After *Revenge of the Creature*, Eastwood would become one of Hollywood's most recognizable leading men, appearing in such films as *The Good, The Bad, and the Ugly* (1967), *Dirty Harry* (1971), and *Unforgiven* (1992).

The team decides to transform it back to a human state by removing its gills and changing the body from scales to a human shape. Lungs are added so it may breathe air. The operation is a success (depending on how you want to look at it), and the Creature becomes fully human and civilized. That is, until yet another beautiful woman happens on the scene. In a bizarre plot twist, the Creature's true nobility is demonstrated as it saves the woman's life from evildoers. However, it yearns to return to the sea and heads sadly and slowly back to the water. But how can it survive in the Black Lagoon without gills to breathe? Will its return result in the Creature's death? The question is never fully answered, as *The Creature Walks Among Us* was the final installment of the Creature series. The movie, and the Creature tales, simply end when we see it walk back out to sea for what would be the final time.

SPOOFING THE CREATURE

The Creature character, however, has appeared elsewhere, making appearances in the monster spoof *Saturday the 14th* (1980) and *The Monster Squad* (1987). The fact that these movies all took place on land made the Creature's appearance that much more outlandish.

Still, even a casual observer today can see the Creature's popularity. The original movie is still considered

The Creature, here played by Don Megowan, is transformed into a human in *The Creature Walks Among Us* (1956), the only one of the three Creature films that was not shot in 3-D.

Tom Woodruff Jr. plays the Gill-man, a spoof on the Creature, in the satire *The Monster Squad* (1987). The film also features comical appearances by Frankenstein, Dracula, the Mummy, and the Wolf Man.

one of the true monster classics (not so much with the two sequels, which many found to be more silly than engaging).

Creature toys, models, and figures were mass-produced to capitalize on the monster's popularity. Today, there are Creature fan clubs devoted to the movie series. The original actors still make the rounds at science-fiction conventions and make personal appearances. Even people who have never seen the movie—since popularized in revivals at local theaters, complete with 3-D glasses—instantly recognize its true star, the girl-crazy, fearsome, reptilian icon.

Strangely, in a movie industry always quick to remake popular old movies, *Creature from the Black Lagoon* is one of the few of the original monster bunch never remade. *The Wolf Man, Dracula, Frankenstein*, and *King Kong* have all appeared in updated (and mostly weaker) remakes of the originals. Many believe that the heart of the Creature's appeal did not lie in its special effects, which were revolutionary at the time. The concept that all "monsters" were not as they appeared has, in fact, fostered the Creature's popularity over the years. The Creature was not a bloodthirsty beast. Rather, it was a phenomenon of nature that only wanted to be left in peace. It is this simple complexity that makes *Creature from the Black Lagoon* one of Hollywood's all-time greatest monster movies.

FILMOGRAPHY

Creature from the Black Lagoon (1954) The movie that launched a monster icon tells the story of a group of scientists bent on finding a reptile man-creature in the waters of South America.

Revenge of the Creature (1955) The sequel once again shows scientists attempting to capture and exploit the mysterious Creature.

The Creature Walks Among Us (1956) In the final installment, the Creature is captured and surgically transformed into a human. Eventually, it escapes and returns to the sea.

GLOSSARY

Academy Award The highest honor awarded to those in the motion picture industry.

amphibian A cold-blooded organism born with gills but that grows to rely on lungs to breathe.

B movie An affectionate term for a low-budget Hollywood movie, most often featuring elements of science fiction.

body mold A frame or shape of a body for use when creating an exact replica; usually constructed of clay or rubber when used in special effects for movies.

cinematographer A person who directs the operation of motion picture cameras.

Devonian Age A prehistoric period of time characterized by the appearance of forests and amphibians.

director The person who controls and supervises a movie.

producer The person who finances a movie production.

spoof A comedic retelling or version of something.

studio Short for movie studio, a business that produces films.

synonymous Something that has a similar meaning as another.

FOR MORE INFORMATION

American Film Institute
2021 N. Western Avenue
Los Angeles, CA 90027-1657
(323) 856-7600
Web site: http://www.afi.com

The Hollywood History Museum
1660 North Highland Avenue
Hollywood, CA 90028
(323) 464-7776
Web site: http://www.hollywoodhistorymuseum.org

WEB SITES
Due to the changing nature of Internet links, the Rosen
Publishing Group, Inc., has developed an online list of Web
sites related to the subject of this book. This site is updated
regularly. Please use this link to access the list:

http://www.rosenlinks.com/famm/mcbl

FOR FURTHER READING AND VIEWING

BOOKS

Garmon, Larry Mike. *Black Water Horror: A Tale of Terror for the 21st Century*. New York: Scholastic, 2002.

Weaver, Tom. *Magicimage Filmbooks Presents Creature from the Black Lagoon* (Universal Filmscripts Series, Classic Science Fiction Films, Vol. 2). Galloway, NJ: Magicimage Filmbooks, 1992.

MOVIES

The Beast from 20,000 Fathoms, directed by Eugene Lourie, Warner Home Video, 1953. DVD.

Creature from the Black Lagoon, directed by Jack Arnold, Universal Studios, 1954. DVD.

The Creature Walks Among Us, directed by John Sherwood III, Universal Studios, 1956. DVD.

King Kong, directed by Ernest Schoedsack and Merian Cooper, RKO Studios, 1933. VHS.

Revenge of the Creature, directed by Jack Arnold, Universal Studios, 1955. DVD.

BIBLIOGRAPHY

Dreadstone, Carol. *Creature from the Black Lagoon.* Berkley,
   CA: Berkley Publishing Group, 1977.
Thorne, Ian. *Creature from the Black Lagoon* (Monster
   Series). Universal City, CA: MCA Publishing: 1981.

INDEX

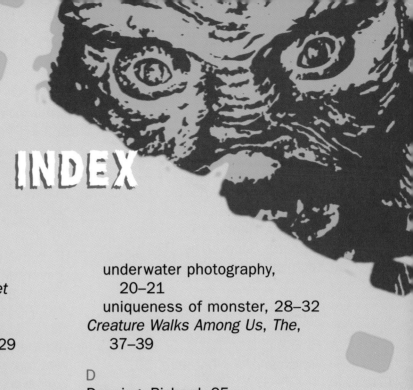

ABOUT THE AUTHOR

Brent Peterson is a writer who lives outside Chicago with his wife, Anne, sons Parker and Maddux, and Daisy the beagle.

PHOTO CREDITS

Cover, pp. 1, 4, 5, 7, 11, 13, 14, 16, 17, 18, 20, 21, 24, 27, 29, 33, 34, 36, 38, 40 © The Everett Collection; p. 22, 30, 31 (left) Bettmann/Corbis; p. 31 (right) © Vo Trung Dung/Corbis Sygma.

Designer: Thomas Forget; Editor: Charles Hofer